Adventure Story Bible
Book 22

Jesus Touches People

Written by Anne de Graaf

Illustrated by José Pérez Montero

Bible Society

Jesus Touches People

Contents — Matthew 14–18; Mark 6–9; Luke 9; John 6

Book 22 — Bible background

The stories in this book took place a little over a year before Jesus was killed. This time is sometimes called the Year of Opposition, because in it Jesus' enemies tried again and again to trap him.

The enemies of Jesus included many religious leaders who felt threatened by the new truths Jesus taught. But Jesus knew what he had to do, and he did not let these people stop him.

Jesus wanted as many people as possible to hear the good news, or gospel. The good news is that those who believe in Jesus can be forgiven for the bad things they have done, and begin instead to live the kind of life Jesus lived, the kind of life God wants us to live. In Jesus' time many of the Jewish religious leaders found this difficult to accept, because it changed the way they understood God.

Again and again Jesus cared for people. He touched their bodies, their minds, and their hearts, making them whole and well. People who follow Jesus today say that he can still do this. Jesus cares for all people.

THE MAN FOR EVERYONE

Jesus is tired

Matthew 14.13; Mark 6.30–33; Luke 9.10; John 6.1–3

Jesus was sad. His friend and cousin, John the Baptist, had just been killed by order of King Herod. As soon as John the Baptist's disciples had buried his body, they ran to tell Jesus the news. They found him, as usual, surrounded by people wanting him to tell them about God, and to reach out and heal them.

They waited until Jesus walked over to them. "Teacher," they said, "John the Baptist has been killed. King Herod's wife, Herodias, wanted him to be killed, and Herod was trapped by her into ordering his death."

John's disciples told him how this had happened. They were all sad, and knew that they had lost a good friend and a good person.

That day the crowds had kept Jesus so busy that he had not even had time to eat. He felt heavy with sadness because his cousin John was dead, and he felt tired.

Jesus called Peter. His closest disciples had just returned from one of their journeys where they had healed and prayed for a great many people. Jesus pointed to a boat on the beach nearby. "Let's go away and rest for a while and be alone," he said.

So Jesus and his disciples went in the boat by themselves to a place where they could be alone.

But the crowd knew that Jesus had gone away somewhere and they tried to find out where. It did not take long before more people than ever crowded the shores of the lake. They left their towns and followed Jesus by land. So when Jesus arrived in the boat a large crowd was waiting for him.

Teaching thousands

Matthew 14.14–15; Mark 6.34–36; Luke 9.11–12
When the boat carrying Jesus and his disciples came to shore, many of the people waded out to meet it. "Jesus! Jesus!" they called to him.

Jesus looked at how many people there were — thousands of them. When he heard them begging him to heal more people who were ill, he welcomed them. His heart warmed with love for all the people. They were like sheep without a shepherd. Because they had no one to lead them, he climbed out of the boat and began teaching them many things.

All that afternoon he told them stories and taught about the love of God. The people sat on the sand and the grass, and listened and watched as Jesus healed the sick and prayed for them.

But as the afternoon wore on, more and more of the people realized how hungry they were. Finally, in the evening, the disciples came to Jesus and said he should send the people away so they could get something to eat in the nearby villages.

Food for the hungry

Matthew 14.16–18; Mark 6.37–38; Luke 9.13;
John 6.4–9

Jesus looked at all the people around him.
They were sitting down, talking in little
groups. The people were excited by all they
had seen and heard that day. He knew that
many were learning, and Jesus still had
something to show them. So he said to Philip,
one of the twelve disciples, "Where can we
buy enough food for all these people?"

Philip was shocked that Jesus would even
suggest such a thing. Philip said, "Why, it
would take everything a man earned for eight
months before we could buy enough food to
feed this many people! Even then they would
only get a few pieces of bread each, certainly
not enough to fill them up."

Then Andrew, Peter's brother, came up to
Jesus. "There is a boy here who has five
loaves of bread and two fish," he said. "But
what use is that when there are thousands of
mouths to feed?"

That is when something quite amazing
happened! When the disciples gave the bread
and fish to the people, they found that there
was enough for everyone! All the thousands
of men, women, and children had enough to
eat.

Then the disciples went around and
collected the bread and fish which were left
over from the meal. When they had finished,
there were twelve baskets of leftovers! How
was that possible, when the two fish and five
loaves Jesus started out with were barely
enough to fill one basket? It was a miracle!

When the people saw this, they could
scarcely believe it. "Not only does he feed us,"
they said, "but he gives us more than we can
eat!"

"How can this Jesus do such strange and
wonderful things?"

"This is truly the prophet we have been
waiting for," they said to each other. They
were amazed by what Jesus had done.

The boy whose lunch fed thousands

Matthew 14.19–21; Mark 6.39–44; Luke 9.14–17;
John 6.10–14

Jesus got all the people to sit in groups. Then
he thanked the boy who had given his bread
and fish to him. Jesus held up the five loaves
and two fish.

Everyone stopped talking. They turned to
watch Jesus. It was not easy for them to be
quiet. They were terribly excited. "What will
happen next?" they whispered to each other.
Jesus thanked God for giving them something
to eat. He blessed the food and broke the
loaves. Then he passed it to the disciples so
they could give it to the people.

FAITH IN ACTION
Learning about faith

Matthew 14.22–24; Mark 6.45–47; John 6.15–18
After Jesus had fed the thousands of people
they said to each other, "Perhaps this is the
one who will become king over us." The Jews
were hoping that Jesus would help them
throw the Romans out of their country.

What they did not understand was that Jesus had not come to earth to rule over it as an earthly king. He came to show that his Kingdom was about love for God and for others, and about making people whole. This was often hard, and involved suffering rather than the life an earthly king would enjoy. The earth does not last for ever, but God's Kingdom will never end. Overthrowing the Romans would not be enough. What the people needed most of all was to live in God's Kingdom and be with him for all time. But the people did not see it that way.

The crowd pushed closer and closer to Jesus. "Let's grab Jesus," many said. "We can force him to become our king, whether or not he wants to."

Jesus knew what the people wanted. But he did not want to become their king on earth. He told his disciples to climb back into the boat they had used to cross Lake Galilee. "Go ahead of me to the other side," he said.

Jesus said goodbye to them, then turned to the crowds. "It's time for you to go home now," Jesus said. Even though there were thousands of them, the people listened.

At last, after Jesus had said goodbye to the crowds, he was alone, without all the people pressing him from every side. He went off by himself and climbed up a hill to pray. It was important for him to spend time alone with his Father. That was how Jesus knew what God wanted him to do. The sun set, and it became very dark.

While Jesus stayed on the hill, praying, the disciples had been trying to cross to the other side of the lake. This was not easy to do in the dark, but several of them were very good fishermen and knew Lake Galilee well.

"I hope we're not in for another storm," Peter said to John. John nodded. He would never forget that terrible night of the storm, when the wild waves had suddenly calmed as soon as Jesus had ordered them to.

"If a storm like that came up tonight we might be in trouble," Peter added. "This time Jesus is not in the boat with us."

As if the weather could read his thoughts, Peter felt the wind change direction. Because the lake was tucked between hills on all sides, the wind could come and go, become strong or weak, in just a matter of minutes. Peter began to worry.

Jesus walks on water

Matthew 14.25–27; Mark 6.48–52; John 6.19–21
By the middle of the night the wind had whipped up and was blowing against them. The disciples strained at the oars, trying to

keep the boat under control as the waves
tossed them about. Jesus saw that the
disciples were in difficulty, so he went to
them. They were still about three or four
miles from shore at this time, and John
shouted, "There's a ghost! Something is
walking on the water!" But it was not a ghost.
The person they saw passing by the boat was
Jesus.

"No, how can it be?" the disciples said to
each other. They were very afraid. With the
wind howling in their ears and the spray
splashing their eyes, they wondered if they
were losing their minds.

But Jesus said, "Don't be afraid! It's me,
Jesus!" The disciples huddled together. They
found it difficult to believe that it was really
Jesus. They were too afraid to believe him.

Peter walks on water

Matthew 14.28–33

The wind roared. The waves formed walls around the boat. Of the little group of scared men, one man stood up. It was Peter. "It is Jesus!" he said to the others. Then he took a step towards the side of the boat and took a closer look.

Jesus' feet barely touched the water, but he did not sink. The waves didn't seem to touch him. Wind blew his hair just as it blew their boat, but Jesus stood upright. He took a step towards the boat. In that instant Peter knew for certain that this was no ghost.

He called out, "Lord, if it is you, tell me to come to you on the water."

Jesus said, "Come on then!"

Peter put one foot over the side, then swung his second leg over and stood up. He did not sink!

He took one step, then another, watching Jesus' face all the time. Peter was walking on water!

But after a few steps, he heard the wind howling. He felt the cold spray on his face. "How can I, just an ordinary fisherman, be walking on water?," he wondered. He started to feel afraid, and then began to sink. "Help! Lord, save me!" he cried out.

Immediately Jesus reached out his hand and grabbed Peter. Jesus said, "Peter, why did you doubt?"

Jesus and Peter climbed into the boat. Once they were safe on board, the wind suddenly stopped. The disciples were astounded, and worshipped Jesus. Not only had they watched Peter walk on water, but Jesus had again been in control of the wind and sea.

Jesus was showing them his power, and they were learning how to trust him.

HEALING AND TEACHING

Many more miracles

Matthew 14.34–36; Mark 6.53–56

When Jesus and his disciples arrived at the far shore the next morning, the men of that village recognized him. "It's Jesus of Nazareth!" they cried out.

They raced in all directions, spreading the word to nearby towns. Soon people were running to the lakeside. The news travelled fast. Jesus had arrived! People from all over the area came to see him, hear him, and touch him.

Sometimes they just touched the bottom of his cloak and they got better, even without Jesus putting his hands on them.

Again they came in great crowds – the sick, the blind, people with skin diseases, and the handicapped. "Heal me!" they asked.

"Teacher, take pity on me!" they said.

"Jesus! Jesus! Over here!" they shouted.

No matter where Jesus went, there were crowds and more crowds. Whether he entered towns or stayed in the countryside, there were always people asking Jesus to heal them.

The bread of life

John 6.22–59

The next day the people who Jesus had fed with the loaves and fish realized that he had

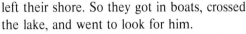

left their shore. So they got in boats, crossed the lake, and went to look for him.

When they found him, Jesus said to them, "You are looking for me because you ate the fish and bread and had all that you wanted. You want to see more miracles, but you don't understand what my miracles mean." The crowd were following him for the wrong reasons.

Jesus explained that he had come to give much more than bread, which eventually turns mouldy. He came to show people God's love and care, and to change their lives. This was real food which would never go mouldy, and always keep people alive.

As Jesus spoke, he made his way to the synagogue in Capernaum. The religious leaders, who didn't like what Jesus was saying and doing, listened to him. Jesus said to the people, "You want something to eat again, as the bread which I gave you a few days ago has not kept you from feeling hungry now. But the new kind of bread which I can give you will keep you from being hungry ever again."

The people wanted to hear more. "Never be hungry?" they asked each other. "How can that be possible?"

The religious leaders said, "Who does he think he is? This is just the son of Mary and Joseph, after all."

But Jesus said, "I am that bread of life. Everyone who comes to me will never go hungry. If they believe in me, they will never be thirsty." Jesus was talking about life with God. Just as we need food to live and make us strong, Jesus was saying, so we also need him. He is the bread from heaven who gives us God's life through the Holy Spirit, so we will live for ever.

The religious leaders mumbled and grumbled. They thought he was lying. "How can he be offering his body to eat?" they asked.

They didn't understand what he was talking about.

Some followers leave Jesus

John 6.60–68

The religious leaders were not the only ones who did not like it when Jesus called himself the bread of life. Many of Jesus' followers questioned this teaching, as well.

"This is too hard," they grumbled to each other.

"We don't understand what he's talking about!" they complained.

Jesus knew they were grumbling and said, "Does this make you want to give up? What I've said to you here is more important than anything else in your life. My words can give you life if you let them."

Then Jesus paused for a moment. He looked at his followers. He knew that some would choose to leave him. They would find it difficult to follow his teaching, so they would go back to their old way of living. "There are some of you here who don't really believe," Jesus said.

When Jesus said this, many of his followers felt as if an arrow had gone straight into their hearts. It was the arrow of truth. Following Jesus wasn't easy. Jesus knew that, so he told the people that they would need God's help.

Several followers turned away then, and left Jesus. They chose not to go with him any more.

Jesus turned to the twelve men who were his closest friends. "Do you want to go away, too?" he asked them.

Peter said, "Lord, where would we go? You have shown us a way to live for ever. We have believed and come to know that you are the Holy One who has come from God."

A clean heart or clean hands?

Matthew 15.1–20; Mark 7.1–13

The Pharisees and teachers of the Law knew the Jewish Law by heart. Some of them who found Jesus difficult were watching him, to catch him out if he did anything wrong.

One day they were standing in the group around Jesus, and they noticed that some of the disciples hadn't washed their hands before eating, as the religious rules said they should.

"Aha!" they said, and asked Jesus, "Why don't your disciples keep our rules about washing hands?"

Then Jesus repeated to them what the prophet Isaiah had written, " 'These people say with their lips that they follow me, using words they don't mean, but their hearts are far away from me.' You would rather hold on to the little rules you have made up and are used to, than think about what God really wanted when he gave Moses the commandments."

Jesus was angry. He called the crowd to him. "Listen to me, all of you, and understand! Which do you think is more important to God, clean hands or a clean heart?

"It's not what you put in your mouth or whether you eat it with clean or unwashed hands that matters."

When Jesus said this, the religious leaders tried to interrupt and stop him. But he went on. "Food doesn't make you good or bad. It's not what goes into you that matters, but how you live. The words you speak and what you do are what's important.

"And the words you speak come from your heart. Keep your heart clean.

"It is from your heart that either good or evil comes, and eating with washed or unwashed hands will not make any difference. Make sure that good comes from your clean heart."

The faith of a foreigner

Matthew 15.21-28; Mark 7.24-30

Jesus knew that he often made the Pharisees angry, but he knew that he was doing and saying what was right, and what God wanted. He had come to tell the good news to the people of Israel. These were the people God chose so long ago when he promised to make Abraham's family into a great nation. He would teach them, and it was their choice whether or not to believe what he said.

God's plan for Jesus at that time was that he should try to teach the people of Israel. Later the good news of God's love would be made known to everyone else in the world.

But while many Jews chose not to believe Jesus, there were other people who were not Jews who did believe in him. One of them was a woman with a little girl who had an evil spirit.

Jesus had travelled to an area near a town called Tyre, where most of the people were not Jews. He was staying at a friend's house and didn't want anyone to know that he was there. But the people living in the village saw him and said, "That is where Jesus, the Jewish teacher, is staying."

This woman went to the house and cried out, "Take pity on me, sir! My daughter has an evil spirit, and is in a terrible condition!"

At first, Jesus didn't say anything, so the woman kept on pleading with him.

His disciples came to Jesus and said, "Send her away. She is making such a lot of noise!"

So Jesus answered the woman, "But I have been sent to work among the Jewish people." The woman rushed over to Jesus and knelt at his feet. "Lord, please help me!" she cried out.

Jesus answered, "It isn't fair to take the children's food and throw it to dogs." In saying this Jesus was trying to explain to the woman that it was God's children, the Israelites, who Jesus had to heal and speak to first.

But the woman said, "Yes, Lord. Yet even the dogs feed on the crumbs which fall from the master's table."

When Jesus heard her answer, he could not turn away from someone who believed in him as strongly as she did, even if she wasn't a Jew.

So he said, "You have great faith! Your daughter is well again, so you can go home now."

The woman did as Jesus told her. At home, she found her little girl asleep in bed. She really was better!

Open ears

Mark 7.31–37

Jesus left that area and returned to Lake Galilee. By that time many more people had heard about how he had fed thousands of people, and was making sick people better. Even though some religious leaders said Jesus was bad, the people could think nothing wrong of him.

Some people brought a friend of theirs to Jesus, begging him to touch the man and make him better. This man could not hear and he had difficulty in speaking.

Jesus took the man aside, away from the crowd. Then he did a very strange thing. He put his fingers into the man's ears. Then he spat and touched the man's tongue.

Jesus looked up towards heaven and took a deep breath. He said to the man, "Be opened!"

And right away the man could hear! He opened his mouth and he could talk normally! The man's friends were utterly astonished. Jesus asked them not to tell anyone about what he had done, but they didn't take any notice. They were so pleased and excited! This news was too good to keep secret.

Everyone who heard about it was completely amazed. "See, everything he does is good. He can even make the deaf hear and those who cannot talk, speak."

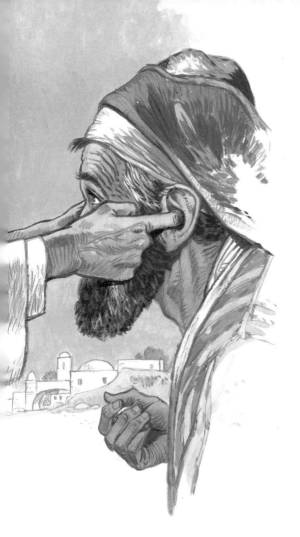

Jesus would not prove who he was by performing a miracle just so they could see it. They had to choose whether to believe him or not. Jesus left them then, and got back into the boat to go to another village on the other side of the lake.

On the way the disciples felt hungry. "Oh no," they said. "We have forgotten to bring enough bread with us! We won't have anything to eat!"

Jesus heard them talking about bread and said to them, "Take care! Be on your guard against the yeast of the Pharisees!" Jesus meant that they should be careful about what the religious leaders taught. In the same way that yeast makes bread, wrong teaching could make people behave the wrong way, and believe the wrong things.

But the disciples were so worried about going hungry they missed Jesus' meaning. "He says this because we don't have any bread," they said.

Jesus explained to them that he was not talking about their food, but about the true bread from God which he had spoken about when he fed the thousands of people, and the false bread of the religious leaders. Then, as if darkness had become light, the disciples knew what Jesus meant. They were to be careful of the Pharisees because they taught things which often weren't helping the people to love and follow God. Jesus, the true bread, led people to God.

What really matters

Matthew 16.1–12; Mark 8.10–21

Jesus left that place and went back across the lake with his disciples. When he arrived at the shore several religious leaders were there to meet him, and they weren't smiling.

"We will not believe you until you perform a miracle for us. Prove that you are who you say you are," they said.

Jesus looked at these men who refused to believe. For over a year he had been healing people and performing miracles in almost every place he visited. Yet these religious leaders still wanted to see more. Jesus sighed, and said, "It is bad to ask for a miracle just for the sake of it, and I will not give you what you want."

A blind man healed at Bethsaida

Mark 8.22-26

Jesus went to a village called Bethsaida. There a group of people brought a blind man to him. "Please, teacher, please just touch our friend, and we know he will get better."

Jesus took the blind man by the hand and led him out of the village.

The blind man did not know what to think as he followed Jesus. He could feel Jesus' hand in his own and it gave him confidence. The blind man had been told by his friends that this was a very holy man. "Jesus has healed others and he can heal you," they had said. But the blind man was not so sure. He desperately hoped that his friends were right.

Jesus stopped, and the blind man felt Jesus take his hand away. Then he heard him spit, and the next thing he knew he felt the warmth of both Jesus' hands against his eyes.

"Do you see anything?" Jesus said.

The man looked up, then he moved his head from side to side and faced Jesus. "I see people, but they look like trees walking about."

Then Jesus laid his hands on the man's eyes again. The man peered and squinted, then began to see everything clearly. A whole new world came alive for him! Colours danced, and soon he saw the smiles of his friends as they greeted him. "I can see! I can see!" he shouted to them. They all gathered around him and hugged him, repeating their thanks to Jesus.

The man wanted to go into the village and tell everybody what had happened. But Jesus asked him not to, and sent him home with his friends. They went on their way full of happiness and thanks to Jesus.

JESUS TEACHES ABOUT HIMSELF

"Who do you think I am?"

Matthew 16.13-20; Mark 8.27-30; Luke 9.18-21

Jesus went with his disciples to the villages north of Lake Galilee, where he spent some time on his own, praying. The disciples came to him, and he asked them a very important question. "Who do people say I am?"

They said, "Some say you're John the Baptist come back to life. Some say you are Elijah, others say Jeremiah or one of the prophets."

Jesus said to them, "Who do you think I am?"

Peter stepped forward. He had to answer for himself, "You are the Messiah, the Son of the living God."

Jesus said to him, "Good for you, Peter! You are specially blessed by God. The only way you could have known that was if my Father in heaven had shown it to you."

Jesus put his hands on his friend's shoulders. "Remember your name Peter," he said.

Peter means "Rock," the kind you can build houses on. Then Jesus went on, "You are a 'Rock', and on this rock foundation I will build my Church. Not even death will mark the end of my Church. I will give you special power and responsibility."

Peter hardly knew what to think. The things Jesus was telling him were hard to imagine. What could it all mean? Despite Peter's confusion, there was one thing he had no doubt about. This man standing before him really was the Son of God.

Just then, as if reading Peter's thoughts, Jesus warned him and the others not to tell anyone who he was. It was not yet part of God's plan for the people to know.

23

Moses and Elijah

Matthew 17.1-9; Mark 9.2-10; Luke 9.28-36

Soon after this, Jesus called Peter and the two brothers James and John. Together they climbed a hill to pray. When they reached the top, Peter, James, and John lay down on the ground and went to sleep.

While they were sleeping, Jesus began to pray. Suddenly, they woke up and saw that Jesus looked very different! Light seemed to beam from Jesus' face, and his clothing became dazzling white.

Then, as if out of nowhere, two men appeared. They were Moses, the man who had led the people of Israel out of Egypt and received the Ten Commandments from God, and Elijah, the greatest prophet! Moses had died a long time ago, and Elijah had disappeared to be with God a long time ago as well. Now they had come back to earth to talk with Jesus.

The three disciples were amazed. "What has happened?" they gasped. They looked at Jesus. He shone like the sun, and their eyes hurt. Then they looked at Moses and Elijah, the two great men who had returned from the past!

They heard Jesus talking about the time coming soon when he would go to Jerusalem and in doing what God wanted, would die there.

Peter wanted this moment on the mountain to last for ever. "Teacher," he said, "this is wonderful! Let us make three tents, one for you, one for Moses, and one for Elijah."

But just then, a bright cloud came over the hill. It was like a white swirling mist around them. A voice came out of the cloud, saying, "This is my Son, my chosen one. Listen to him!"

The disciples were terrified. They fell face down on to the ground.

When the voice stopped, Jesus came to them and said, "It's all right. You can get up now. There's no reason to be afraid."

Only then did the disciples dare to look. Slowly, they opened their eyes. They saw Jesus, no longer looking bright as the sun, standing before them. The cloud had gone, and Moses and Elijah had disappeared, too.

Later, as the three followed Jesus down the hill, he told them they were not to tell anyone what they had seen. Jesus said it would be a secret until after he had risen from the dead. Peter, James, and John did not know what he meant by this, and discussed it with each other. But they couldn't understand it. They would wait and see what happened.

Just a little faith

Matthew 17.14–21; Mark 9.14–29; Luke 9.37–43

When Jesus, Peter, James, and John reached the bottom of the hill, they returned to the other disciples. As they came near, they saw that a crowd had gathered. Some of the religious leaders were arguing with Jesus' disciples.

As soon as the crowd saw Jesus walking toward them, they cried out, "There's Jesus, he'll know what to do!" And they ran towards him.

"What is going on?" Jesus asked them.

A man said, "Teacher, I brought my son to your disciples, but they could not help him. He cannot talk, and sometimes he has epileptic fits. I asked your disciples to make him better, but they couldn't."

Jesus said to the people, "You still don't believe, do you? How much longer will I have to put up with you?" There was so much more they needed to learn from Jesus.

Jesus turned to the boy's father and asked, "How long has he been like this?"

"Since childhood. Sometimes he even throws himself into fire or water. I am so afraid he will die or hurt himself badly. Please, if you can do anything, help us!" he said.

Jesus looked at the man. "If you can have faith in me, I can heal the boy," he said. "Everything is possible for the person who has faith."

The man wanted to believe in Jesus more than anything, but it wasn't easy. "I do want to believe you, but it's so hard," he said. "Please help me not to doubt any more."

This was what Jesus was waiting for. He wanted the father to understand the importance of believing in what he asked, and to want to believe in him. That is what it means to have faith.

26

The boy was brought to Jesus, and had a fit right there. Even as he was on the ground, Jesus healed the boy. But he lay so still afterwards, many were afraid he might be dead.

Jesus leant over and took the boy's hand. He eased him on to his feet and handed him over to his father. The father couldn't say anything, he was so happy to have his son well again.

After the man and his son left, Jesus' disciples asked him why they hadn't been able to heal the boy. "You didn't have enough faith. All you need is faith no bigger than a grain of mustard seed. With that you could even tell a mountain to move, and it would. You needed to pray with faith and power."

Jesus speaks about his suffering

Matthew 17.22–23; Mark 9.30–32; Luke 9.43–45

One day, as Jesus and his disciples passed through a crowd, they overheard the people talking about how great God was.

Jesus turned to his disciples. "Don't forget what I am about to tell you. Let these words sink in. Now the people talk about God's greatness, but it will not be long before the Son of Man is handed over to men who will kill him. But three days later he will come alive again."

The disciples did not know what Jesus meant. They knew it was an important message about Jesus, the Son of Man, but they were filled with grief and too afraid to ask about it.

Jesus and the disciples left the crowd behind. This was a time for Jesus to teach his disciples, and he wanted to be alone with them. These men would carry on Jesus' teaching after he died and he had to prepare them for the job. Time was running out.

GOD'S WAY IS DIFFERENT

The fish with a coin in its mouth

Matthew 17.24-27

In Capernaum, a man who collected taxes for the Jewish Temple came to Peter and said, "Does your teacher pay the temple-tax?"

This was a tax which all Jews had to pay to the religious leaders. It was worth two days' wages, which was a lot of money. Peter said to him, "Of course Jesus pays it." Then he went into the house where Jesus was staying.

Before Peter had a chance to tell Jesus about it, Jesus asked him, "What do you think, Peter? When a king makes people pay taxes, should the ones who pay be those from his own family and country, or the foreigners who are living on his land?"

"Only the foreigners should pay," Peter said.

"Yes, so the Jews should not have to pay temple-tax, because they are not foreigners in their own Temple. But so that no one gets angry over something which doesn't matter much, we will pay the tax."

Jesus said, "Go down to the lake and go fishing. Take the first fish that comes up. When you open its mouth you will find a coin worth enough to pay my temple-tax and yours."

Become like children

Matthew 18.1–14; Mark 9.33–37; Luke 9.46–48

One day while the disciples were walking with Jesus, they were arguing — quietly so that Jesus wouldn't hear — about which one of them was the most important.

Later, Jesus asked his twelve closest disciples, "What were you arguing about on the way?"

Even though they were a bit ashamed to answer, they said, "We wanted to know which of us will be the most important person in God's Kingdom."

There was a child playing nearby. Instead of answering his disciples, Jesus called the child over and stood him by his side. "Do you see this little one?" he asked. "The one who can become like a child, trusting and humble, that person will be the most important in God's Kingdom.

"Whoever takes care of children and teaches them about me, has also welcomed me. But people who hurt children, or teach them not to trust in me, will be in terrible trouble. It would be better for them if a huge stone were tied around their necks and someone threw them into the sea!"

His friends shivered at the thought and looked at the child, who was now sitting on Jesus' lap.

Jesus said, "Take care of children and love them."

Jesus told them that in order to have a special place in God's Kingdom, they would have to stop thinking of themselves all the time. Other people must come first, especially those like children, who aren't important or powerful.

Not alone

Matthew 18.15–22

Jesus carried on telling the disciples that it was not only the children they must love, but the people who did wrong to them.

"But what if somebody cheats us? What if someone is doing something really wrong?" Jesus' disciples asked him.

Jesus told them that whenever someone hurts them, they should first go to that person alone and gently see if they can help make things right again. "If that doesn't work, then take friends with you and talk about it. But don't be angry," he said. Only when the person refuses to admit they are wrong should you talk about them with the church.

Then Jesus taught them about what it would be like after he died. Jesus' disciples would have Jesus' power on earth. They would be the ones who would help to give God's forgiveness. "Whenever two of you agree about anything you pray for, your Father in heaven will listen and answer your prayer," Jesus said.

"But we don't want you to go," they said. Panic seized them at the thought of Jesus dying.

Jesus smiled at them and said, "It's all right. Remember, I'm always going to be with you. Whenever two or more of you come together, I'll be listening. I will be right there with you."

That is a promise Jesus made to all his followers, for all time.

Adventure Story Bible

Old Testament

New Testament